The Clouds Will Catch Me

The Clouds Will Catch Me

Cori Sykes

Write and Vibe Publishing
Cleveland

Copyright © 2020 by Cori Sykes

All rights reserved. No part of this publication may be reproduced, distributed, or transmitted in any form or by any means, including photocopying, recording, digital scanning, or other electronic or mechanical methods, without the prior written permission of the publisher, except in case of brief quotations embodied in critical reviews and certain other noncommercial uses permitted by copyright law. For permission requests, please address Write and Vibe.

This publication contains the opinions and ideas of its author. The author has tried to recreate events, locales, and conversations from memory. In order to maintain anonymity, names of individuals and places or identifying characteristics and details such as physical properties, occupations and places of residence may have been changed. Any resemblance to actual persons or organizations, living or dead, is purely coincidental.

Edited by Lyrical Innovations, LLC

Published 2020
Printed in the United States of America
ISBN: 978-1-953430-03-8 (pbk)
ISBN: 978-1-953430-04-5 (ebook)
Library of Congress Cataloging-in-Publication Data is available.

For information, address:
Write and Vibe Publishing
P.O. Box 201372
Cleveland, OH 44120
cori@writeandvibe.com

This book is dedicated to my mother, Karen Todd, who served as my loudest cheerleader, to my sister, Dani, who walked this journey with me, and to my family, Lamar, Amani and Cara, who continue to light up my life.

I am forever grateful for my crew.

Introduction

"Do you miss me?" Ma would ask.

"No." My answer was always the same. I, her oldest daughter, would joke that she never left long enough for me to miss her.

She would then inject her contagious cackle into our conversation until I either hung up or handed the phone to someone else. This was our tradition. Every single time.

I miss my mom now and have missed her since she died on Sunday, October 14, 2018.

Since her death, there are many things that I have wished for. I wish I would've hugged her the night I left her room for the last time. I wish I could forget the call that broke the horrible news. I wish the hospital would have had an updated phone number for them to reach me. I wish I wasn't forced to find a new normal. But none of these things are possible. They are all pieces of my journey that I must work through.

This story, this work that you're about to read, is a part of me working through the wishes that can't be granted. It is a very brief stagger through a period of time that I felt would not end. Although this is a compacted version, please understand that the storyline remains intact. This is simply my attempt to continue healing and processing Ma's abrupt physical departure from our lives. A loss that left my sister and me feeling like orphans.

It's also meant to, prayerfully, provide Ma's loving extended family and coworkers a little semblance of peace. You see, Ma loved her God faithfully and, while cleaning her apartment, I found her prayer notebook. Throughout *The Clouds Will Catch Me,* you will read bits of her prayers and see that, although her death caught us off guard, God was standing at the ready, waiting to receive her.

Lastly, if you lost a loved one while they were in the care of a hospital or nursing home, this story may trigger painful memories or thoughts. If you find that you are unable to continue reading this at any point, please put the book down. Believe me, there were many times while writing this that I had to put the book down. Therapy has helped but there are still days when I figuratively *put down my book*, and that's okay.

"Lord, thank you for guiding me the way you want me to go."
Karen Todd

he refreshes my soul. He guides me along the right paths for his name's sake.
Psalms 23:3

Thursday, October 4, 2018

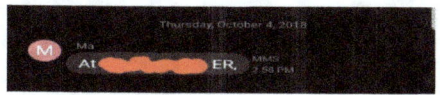

I dragged my eyes from my computer monitor to my phone, which was buzzing lightly on my desk. An involuntary groan escaped my throat. There are a minimal amount of people who were able to irritate me in a single text and Ma was definitely one of them.

I studied her message, blinking my eyes every few seconds, waiting for something more to come through. But there was nothing. No explanation. No *LOL*. No *9-1-1*. The only thing I knew was she was at Gateway hospital in the emergency room. I blew a dose of irritated air from my lungs in order to calm myself before dialing her number.

"Hey," she answered.

Her voice didn't sound out of the norm, so I kept it cool. "Hey, what's going on? Why are you in the ER?"

"Well…" she took a deep breath, "they think I'm having a stroke."

A friend of mine once posted a meme on social media saying, *God bless the daughter with a Capricorn mother*. At that moment, I felt the meaning of that post in my soul. Ma was a Capricorn and I was definitely an impatient and easily irritated Aries.

"Your job thinks you're having a stroke?"

"No, I was off today. The hospital staff thinks I'm having a stroke, but they have to do some tests."

My finger tapped my desk like a woman waiting for her barista to get her second order of coffee right. Was this an emergency or not? "Why do they think it's a stroke?"

"Because I can't open my left hand and I can barely move my left leg."

Paralysis on one side of her body read stroke to me. It also read *emergency* but she spoke as if she were lying on a park bench watching lovers pass. "Yeah, that sounds like a stroke. But wait…" I straightened in my chair, "if you weren't at work, how'd you get to the hospital? Who took you?"

As a single empty nester, Ma had zero interest in ride-sharing, calling taxis, or taking the bus. All of that added up to one thing.

"I drove here."

I leaned over my desk and rested my forehead in my palm. "You drove yourself to a hospital over thirty minutes away even though you thought you were having a stroke? Why would you do that? You could have passed out and killed yourself. Or someone else."

With her voice lowered, she answered, "I know. I wasn't thinking. I just wanted to get here."

I started running my fingers through my hair, a horrible habit that I wouldn't be breaking anytime soon. "Ma, you should've called an ambulance."

"I know."

"Is Dani up there with you?" I asked, referring to my sister.

"She's at work."

"Okay, I'll be there soon. Bye." Her lack of protest proved how scared she truly was. Still, I kept my cool until I could determine the gravity of the situation. With Ma, it could be nothing, or it could be *everything*.

I headed to the next cubicle over to talk to my supervisor, knocking lightly on the divider.

He spun away from his computer, placing his hands on his lap. "Heyyy, what's up?"

I looked into his glasses, laughing inwardly as I pushed mine up my nose. He never seemed to need to adjust his. Perfect fitting, I guess. Then I thought of how it was an

Cori Sykes

awkward thing to think of at such an urgent time. I needed to get my life together.

"I need to leave. My mom just sent me a text saying she's in the emergency room."

"Oh no," he straightened in his seat and crossed one leg over the other. He was a thin, younger man. The couple pictures of his family and his paper-free desk proved he also preferred the simple life.

"Yeah, the doctors think it's a stroke. I just talked to her and she sounds fine, but I still need to go check on her."

"Sure, family first. Take all the time you need."

I chuckled, "I'm sure she's fine but, thank you. I'll see you tomorrow."

He smiled, "All right."

I walked back to my desk and sat for a second, taking in the pictures of my daughters on my desk. If nothing else made me smile, they always could. Both were comedic spitfires in their own way, and they kept my husband, Lamar, and me on our toes.

Since we worked for the same company, I sent Lamar an instant message, letting him know I was leaving for the day. He responded immediately. Sensing that he was nervous and concerned, I assured him that Ma was fine.

With it nearing dinner time, I called Ma when I got closer to the hospital.

"Hello."

Her voice still sounded normal enough, making me smile with relief. "Hey, Ma. I should be there in about twenty minutes but since it's almost five, did you want me to pick you up something to eat? Or will they be releasing you soon?"

Ma sighed. "As far as I know, I'll be here for at least a few more hours. I'm waiting for an MRI and they're doing other blood tests to see what's causing the paralysis."

I rolled my eyes. As much as I loved doctors, I also thought they were a crockpot of shit. "They still don't know why you can't move the left side of your body? I'm no doctor but if you can't move one side of your body it clearly sounds like a stroke."

"I know. Same thing I was thinking."

"Doctors are idiots. What did you want me to get you to eat?"

"Are you near a Subway?"

"Even if I wasn't, I'd still get it for you. Text me your order."

"I want a veggie delight on..."

"Ma," I interrupted. "You gotta text me what you want on it. That's a lot to remember."

"I just want a six-inch on Italian bread. All the veggies except I want spinach instead of lettuce."

I calmed my frustration, realizing it could be difficult to text with one hand. "Okay, six-inch veggie on Italian with spinach instead of lettuce," Ma confirmed as I pulled into a parking spot. "No dressing or cheese?"

"Nope."

"Okay, bye."

"Bye, and thank you."

"You're welcome."

A short car ride later, I pulled into the ER parking lot, blasting music that filled my eardrums with cursing and debauchery. I sang every word at the top of my lungs until my voice turned raspy and I had to turn the music down. When I glanced out the window, I noticed Ma's car two spaces down and, just like that, the situation went from fun to very real. I bit the corner of my lip to keep it from quivering.

Even if Ma didn't let on, she was in a fragile state and she didn't need me scaring her. I could be weak later but now wasn't the time. Plus, I didn't want to jump to conclusions. There was still a possibility that she could go home that night.

"Be strong. No tears. Make her laugh. Act normal," I chanted all the way inside, stopping after walking through the sliding doors. Undecorated grey walls greeted me as I entered. A quick glance around showed employees reclining in chairs and checking cell phones.

"I'm here to see Karen Todd," I spoke to the receptionist. "She came in a few hours ago."

The receptionist, a talkative young woman with animated hands, spun around to face me. "Are you related?"

"I'm her daughter."

She pushed over the sign-in sheet. "Sign in." She then went back to her conversation with the security guard next to her. "She was acting all rude, flipping her hands and staring me down. I'm not the one. She think she scare me? Nah."

I did as I was told, then her long nail tapped a small plastic blue basket. "Put your purse in here and go through the metal detector," she pointed behind me, never losing track of her conversation.

I turned around and stepped through. *This* was their security system? One random metal detector in the middle of an empty hallway. I could just as easily walk around than go through and they wouldn't be the wiser. I walked on through and dropped my arms. "Is that it?"

The receptionist waited for confirmation from the security guard, who was looking through my purse. When he nodded, she pushed the button, unlocking the doors to the hospital ER entrance. "Yeah, here's your purse. Your mom is straight back."

I grabbed my purse with the Subway sandwich inside. When the doors opened, I immediately saw Ma reclined on a bed. Just sitting there. Her expression proved she wouldn't be winning any awards for Happiest Person of the Year.

Ma looked up from her toes and noticed me, but didn't smile. "Hey."

I repeated my chant. *Be strong. No tears. Make her laugh. Act normal.* "Hey! Brought your food." I handed over her sandwich and took a seat in the only empty chair in the room. Barely bigger than a closet, the room thankfully allotted for a TV that remained off. Besides the beeping of the machines monitoring her heart rate and other vitals, all was quiet.

"You don't wanna watch TV? The remote is right next to you."

She looked to where I pointed. "I hadn't even noticed." Ma glanced away, placing her sandwich on the tray next to her. "You can turn it on if you want but I'm fine."

I nodded through her melancholy. "You're not hungry?"

"I can't eat until they do this scan."

"When are they supposed to do the scan?"

"I don't know. They were supposed to do it over an hour ago but there's a schedule and I guess they're behind." She shrugged.

I glanced into the hallway. Nurses were talking everywhere and the only indication of work getting done was one nurse typing on a computer.

"You think my feet look swollen?"

I looked back at her and stood up for a closer look. "Umm, maybe. Did you mention it to the doctors here?"

"No."

"Why not?"

"I don't know."

"I think you should tell them. Just so they are aware."

She didn't bother agreeing. I knew she wouldn't tell the doctors unless she felt it was relevant to her current situation. I knew she would deal with it as she always did, so I changed the subject.

"I know you said Dani is at work, but were you able to let her know that you're here?"

"Yeah, I text her. She was mad that I drove up here, too."

I raised my eyebrows. "For obvious reasons."

Just when I was about to sit back down, a taller, brown-haired male nurse came in. He spoke to Ma as if they'd attended parties together back in college. "Heyyy, Karen. I'm here to take you for your scan, but first, do you have to use the restroom? Don't wanna be up getting your scan and then realize you gotta go. That would be just terrible."

"Yeah, I could go."

"All right! Think you can walk there?"

"Yeah."

He nodded and moved to help her up, but then looked closer at the hospital bands around her wrist. "Your bracelet says *Fall Risk*. Are you at risk of a fall, Ms. Karen?"

I sat down and crossed my arms, waiting to interject. I knew that Ma would insist on being her independent self.

"Well," she started. "I fell the other day, trying to get in bed. My doctor says I have arthritis in both knees."

The nurse leaned to the left to disconnect her cords from the machine. "And you think you can walk?"

Ma pointed across the hallway. "It's right there, so I should be fine."

My impatient foot bounced on the ground and he looked as if he were about to let her walk over there by herself. There was no way I was about to let her do that when using a wheelchair was safer.

"She should not be walking," I spoke up. He turned to me and nodded. "She's fallen more than a few times. Her leg is pretty much paralyzed from this potential stroke and her ankles are swollen."

He looked back at Ma. "Darling, we don't want you falling. How about I get a wheelchair, just to be safe? And then we'll go get you scanned. That sound okay?"

Ma nodded and then looked at me. She said nothing and I couldn't help but speak again. "I just don't want you falling. Would hate to add broken bones to your list of ailments."

She huffed and shook her head while waiting for the nurse to return. By the time she came back, the hospital had decided to admit her and had already gotten a room prepared.

In her personal room, Ma asked, "How long will I be here?"

"I don't know yet," the young nurse smiled and covered Ma with a blanket. "Tomorrow you'll see the doctor and he'll go over everything. You'll know more then."

Once the nurse exited the room, I walked over to Ma's bed and put everything she would need within arm's reach. "You want me to send a group text to the family?"

Ma had three living sisters, one brother, and two sisters-in-law. Add in seven nieces and nephews and the family was a large body to notify.

"Not really, but go ahead."

I didn't bother asking for clarification. I just nodded and proceeded with the group text. "Since you'll be here for a little while…"

"Hopefully not that long," Ma interrupted. I didn't blame her for wanting to leave already.

"Yeah, hopefully not that long. But since we at least know you'll be here overnight, do you need me to get anything from your place or take anything there?"

The Clouds Will Catch Me

I typed her requests on my phone's notepad and prepared for a longer than expected night. It would be at least two hours before I made it home and it was already after eight.

When I returned to the hospital, later that evening, Ma's energy had drastically decreased. Her face hung low and her eyes drooped. She looked burned out. Exhausted. Her mouth remained fixed in a constant line and she spoke as if the devil had burned all the life right out of her body.

"Hey." No wave. No smile. Barely a blink. Her hospital gown hardly rose and fell, indicating she was alive. "Got everything you needed." I held up the bag and began to empty the contents onto the tray in front of her. "I got all the books and I even brought a few from home, too. And a word search. Do you like those?"

"Not really."

"Okay, well I'll leave it here anyway, just in case you get bored. Remember I used to do those with Grandma?"

She nodded, not even smiling from the memories of me with her mother. "Thanks."

"You're welcome. I'm gonna sit with you a little longer because I may not be here tomorrow, if that's okay. You know tomorrow is Silk's birthday and I still need to pick up a few things." I'd tried to prepare for my husband's birthday that year like a dutiful wife, but shit had hit the fan.

"That's fine."

"Oh, and I talked to Nicky. He's out of the hospital and doing better. Crazy, right?"

Nicky, my biological father, had been in and out of the hospital over the past two weeks. Up until a couple of days prior, the doctors hadn't known what was wrong with him. He lived out of state and, although he'd been absent since I was an infant, there was no bad blood between him and Ma, as far as I knew.

"Wow." Her excitement didn't quite convince me that she was interested in or concerned about my father's status.

"I know." I smirked before adding, "And he said to tell you to get better soon." I waited for a larger amount of emotion to surface, but all I got was a slight lift of her mouth. "I told him y'all are in cahoots to drive me crazy. First, he goes into the hospital and almost dies. Then as soon as he gets out, you go in. It's a conspiracy I tell ya. If I didn't know any better, I'd say y'all been talking behind my back on the phone."

Ma's face scrunched up and she adjusted in bed. Finally, a reaction. "I don't want him."

"Sure, you don't."

I stayed a little longer before promising to return in a couple of days with my daughters.

They were asleep when I got home. I felt my way through the darkness and up the stairs, fully expecting Lamar to be asleep. Instead, he lifted his head from the pillow and watched me close our bedroom door. His eyes squinted under the TV light.

"How is she?"

After hearing those three little words, I crumbled into his arms. Careful not to wake our oldest daughter, Amani, I sobbed deeply. "She looks tired...like she's given up. I'm scared."

"Lord, help me to be more frugal, more loving, more understanding. Give me the wisdom to know what to say and when to honor you. Lord, help me to see the God in people."
Karen Todd

And we know that in all things God works for the good of those who love him, who have been called according to his purpose.
Romans 8:12

Saturday, October 6, 2018

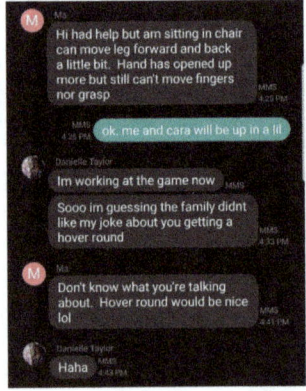

"Aww," a floor nurse cooed. "It's so nice to see babies here. She's so precious."

The elevator doors closed behind my youngest daughter, Cara, and me. In front, Cara waddled, leading the way to Ma's room as I replied, "Thank you."

When Cara turned the wrong way, I redirected her. "This way, baby."

Cara screeched and caught back up with me.

"I thought that was you." Ma sat up straight in her bed with a pillow pushed behind her neck.

"What gave us away?" I chuckled as I took a seat in the chair next to the bed. "Say hi to Grandma," I pointed to Ma.

Cara refused with a whine, so I pulled her into my lap. "Stop treating Grandma like that. You're gonna need her one day."

"That's right," Ma wagged her finger, "and I'll remember how badly you treated me."

Cara snuggled closer to me and started sucking her thumb.

"Is that your dinner over there on the tray?" Ma glanced at it, then looked away, frowning slightly. "Yeah, but I don't want it. It's nasty. Cara can have the flavored ice."

"You sure you don't want it? Did you eat anything today?" Ma shrugged, "Yeah, I ate breakfast. I just don't have much of an appetite."

"Do the doctors know that?" Ma wasn't small by any means. The only thing small on her was her height and her tiny head. Although she boasted about being a light eater, Ma could put away some food.

My brain spun in circles and my eyebrows moved closer together. I already knew the answer and I hated that she often kept things from her doctors. Ma huffed and shrugged. I got up from the chair to place a bib around Cara's neck. Right as I sat down, a knock came from the door.

"Hi, Ms. Karen. I'm here to give you a breathing treatment. Is now a good time or do you want me to come back?" The respiratory therapist glanced between us.

"Now is fine."

I watched closely as the respiratory therapist emptied the medicine in a small tube and flipped the switch to start the vapors. Ma breathed in the vapors, training her eyes on the TV while the medicine evaporated into her lungs.

Once the treatment was complete, I reclined in the chair. Upon noticing that her paralyzed leg was sticking out, I asked, "You want me to cover your leg? Are you cold?"

She removed her mouthpiece. "I'm fine. Look at this though." Ma wiggled her big toe. It barely moved, but it was something. "And look at this, too." She held out her hand. "It's opened more."

I inspected her foot and hand. Though I was happy to see her progress, I preferred that she wasn't in that position at all. I slowly bobbed my head and repositioned Cara in the seat next to me. "That's really great. I wonder how long it'll take for you to get back to normal. Your leg is still swollen, too. Did you ever ask the doctor what's causing that?"

Ma shrugged it off. "I'm just happy to not be having spasms anymore. They were so bad last night I was in tears. Crying out. And it took the nurse forever just to get me some pain meds."

"Didn't the same thing happen the night before?"

"Well, the spasms did but it didn't take long to get medicine."

I officially hated this hospital. "I feel like every time I come, they've done something wrong. And their bedside manner is not the best. I mean, what else could they possibly be doing in the middle of the night? They were probably asleep. Do you know what the process is to get you moved to another hospital?"

"You won't need to do that because my insurance finally approved me to go to a rehabilitation center."

"That's good." I smiled at her before looking back down at my phone.

"And I met with the neurologist. He said I didn't have a stroke on Thursday, but I did have one recently."

"What? So you're saying the symptoms you're having now are from an old stroke? I never even knew that was possible."

"Me neither."

"Did you ever find out why your insurance denied coverage for your stay at the other facility?"

"They say the program was too intensive and they didn't think I'd be able to withstand therapy twice a day."

I put my phone back down and stared at her. "If your doctors didn't think you'd be successful at the rehabilitation place, they wouldn't have recommended it."

"That's what I thought."

I extended my legs and stretched my arms before remembering I was supposed to be grabbing the flavored ice for Cara. "So, I'm guessing you wouldn't have to do all that at this new place."

"I guess not," Ma huffed.

We sat in silence before I said, "Well, at least you're finally getting outta here. When are you supposed to go and what's the name of the place?"

"I don't have a date yet. I'm waiting to see if they have a bed for me. It's called Circle of Angels and it's in the City of Mandover."

"Okay, that's good. It's not far. This is really good news. Means you're strong enough to leave."

"Yeah." Ma concentrated on her hands and said nothing further, so I switched gears. "Hey, would you be up to do a live video on Facebook? That way, the family can see that you're okay. I won't put your face or anything in the video. It's just so they can hear your voice. I think they're worried."

"Yeah, that's fine." While I pulled out my cell phone, Ma placed her tubes on the table next to her.

"Okay, cool." I opened Facebook and started our live feed.

Note: The below QR Code will take you to the last video of Ma. Alternatively, you can go to https://genuinelyeverafter.com/hospital-video/

"Lord, thank you for healing my body of impurities."
Karen Todd

The human spirit can endure in sickness, but a crushed spirit who can bear?
Proverbs 18:14

Wednesday, October 10, 2018

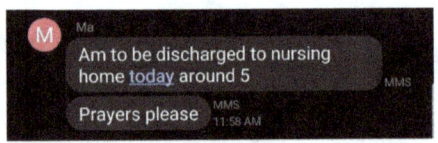

Right on schedule, two male paramedics walked into Ma's hospital room with a stretcher. Happy to see the beginning of the end of Ma's rehabilitation journey, I found myself smiling at her, despite her blank stare.

"Ms. Karen?" The first guy folded a piece of paper and shoved it into his back pocket.

"Yes," Ma twisted her fingers around each other, then abandoned that motion and gripped her bed sheets.

"You ready to get outta here?"

"A little nervous," she admitted.

I bit the inside of my cheek. I had a feeling her nervousness dealt more with not wanting to put in the work to get better versus being concerned about the safety of the facility.

"Why are you nervous?" The first man asked.

Ma's head leaned ever so slightly. "How are they there? Are they nice?"

"They're really nice," the second man chimed in. "We take patients there all the time."

"So, you've been there before?"

"Oh yeah," the first man spoke again. "We're there almost every day, either taking or picking up patients."

One thing I could always count on was for Ma's dramatics to worry everyone unnecessarily. "Ma, relax. You're not the first person to have a stroke and to have to go to rehab. You'll be fine."

"They'll take good care of you there," the first man assured her as they belted her onto the stretcher. "When we drop off patients, there's always a person at the front desk. At some places, the employees either run from us or we have to go find someone. I like it at Circle of Angels."

"See, they know what they're talking about." I placed Ma's purse near her feet and gave her a reassuring smile that, once again, wasn't returned. "It'll be cool, Ma. Nothing to worry about. I'm gonna go to my car and I'll meet you there."

I blasted my music all the way to Circle of Angels. The world was a much lighter load with both of my parents released from their respective hospitals. And the inside of the Circle of Angels facility was everything I would have paid for if Ma's insurance wasn't footing the bill. Its community rooms, well-tended residents, and sparkles of cleanliness welcomed me.

When I got to her room, Ma had already changed into a fresh gown. "This looks nice, Ma." Though her room was smaller, there was plenty of space to fit the attached bathroom, armoire, TV, and a bulletin board with a calendar of activities. "How much is this costing your insurance?" I joked as I sat down in a chair at the foot of her bed.

"From what I gather, it's a lot. But not as expensive as those in assisted living because I don't need 'round the clock help'." Ma lowered into her gossip voice. "And get this, the person across the hall from me has already been screaming his head off, talking about, 'Nurse! Nurse'!" She smacked her lips. "He's already on my nerves and I just got here." "Hopefully he'll shut up soon. I'm not gonna stay long. Just wanted to make sure you got in alright."

"Mm-hmm," she sniffed.

Right when I was about to mention the bulletin, one of her nurses breezed into the room and right past me with papers.

The Clouds Will Catch Me

"Ms. Karen. I have the pharmacy on the phone and they're saying you're allergic to one of the ingredients in this medicine." She pointed to the paper.

Ma looked at it closely. "I don't know why they're saying that. I've been taking that for years."

"And you haven't had any reactions to it?" asked the nurse

"Nope. I mean, not that I know of. I take it all the time."

I closely watched their interaction. It seemed every time I turned around, Ma was on new medication. The amount of meds she was on grew to be so high that I wasn't sure how she kept up with them all. As far as I knew, her only ailment was high blood pressure and arthritis, so all of the other medications that were being mentioned were news to me.

"So, you want me to tell them to go ahead and fill it?" the nurse confirmed.

"Yes," Ma nodded. As quickly as she had come in, the nurse walked back out.

I pointed to the bulletin over my head. "You see they have BINGO? You should go. Maybe make some friends," I smirked and Ma rolled her eyes.

"I'm not making friends with any of those people. Hopefully I won't be here that long."

"You better quit playing. You never know, your next husband may be at the table next to you making eyes at you over his BINGO card. You better get you a sugar daddy." We hadn't bantered like that in a while and I was enjoying myself.

"I can't stand you. I start physical therapy and occupational therapy tomorrow, so can you get me some clothes from my apartment?"

"What all do you need?"

"A couple of comfortable shirts, pants, and some sneakers. And oh," she added an afterthought, "maybe a scarf, since I don't have my wigs here."

"You got it."

"Today, I will have happy and hopeful thoughts. Optimism will be my companion, victory, my hallmark."
Karen Todd

Cori Sykes

For the Lord takes delight in his people; he crowns the humble with victory.
Psalms 149:4

Saturday, October 13, 2018

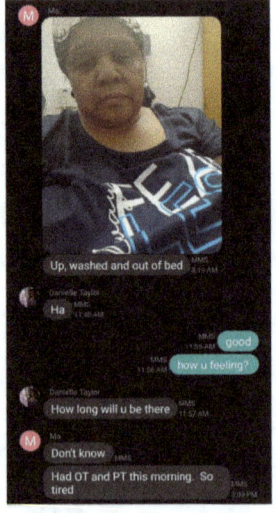

"Heyyy!"

Ma's eyes diverted to Amani and me. Her lowered voice was an indication of her ever-gossiping self. "I'll call you back later. Cori and Amani just walked in."

I couldn't help chuckling. "Always gossiping."

"Right," Amani hugged Ma.

"Oh hush," she waved us off while we found a place to sit. "What y'all up to?"

"Coming to see you. How are you feeling?"

"Tired. Therapy is kicking my butt, but I know I have to do it in order to get out of here."

She didn't look as tired as when she was first admitted to the hospital and certainly seemed to be on the up and up. I said, "Well, you look better. What all do they have you doing?"

"I've been exercising and trying to get my knees stronger. I'm also working on picking up things with my two fingers." She motioned to her gimp hand with her head. "It's harder than I thought. I appreciate little things like that much more."

"I bet."

"And then last night I didn't sleep too good. I had bad indigestion and was throwing up. They finally gave me some Milk of Magnesia after I kept asking."

"What'd you eat that upset your stomach?" I made a mental note in my head, but did not get hung up on it. Ma would often cough herself into a vomiting episode.

"Nothing I can think of. Haven't had much of an appetite. Plus, this food is nasty."

"Well, you have to eat something. There's nothing here that you like? Maybe I can bring you something. Are you on a special diet?"

"Yeah, that's why it's nasty."

"Okay, well I guess we won't be bringing you any food then. You have to eat something, though. You'll be outta here soon and able to eat real food again," I said.

"Yeah, yeah. How's my baby doll?" she officially ended the conversation and focused on Amani, who was now standing next to her bed.

"Good."

"Good, huh? High school still stressing you out?"

"Yeah, Grandma, tell me why my teacher gave us a pop quiz on Friday?"

"I don't know. Why?"

I chuckled at their exchange and started switching the stations on the TV. "That was rhetorical, Ma."

"What kinda teacher gives pop quizzes on Fridays?" Amani continued.

"I don't know."

I shook my head and laughed again. "Another rhetorical question, Ma. Oh look, *Hocus Pocus* is on!" The smile on my face could have brightened any room. As kids, Dani and I had recorded countless movies on VHS and watched them relentlessly on weekends and during summer break. *Hocus Pocus* was one of them.

"Your mom and auntie loved this movie," Ma explained as Amani tied Ma's scarf around her head and reclaimed her seat.

"You don't mind if we watch this, do you?"

Ma shook her head. Halfway through the movie, a woman I assumed to be an administrator walked in. Although she still wore scrubs, her relaxed demeanor suggested her job was less stressful. "Karen, is this your daughter? Cori?"

I responded, "Yes."

"Oh good." She adjusted her glasses and flipped the page on her clipboard. "I'm glad you're here. I need to set up a meeting with you to discuss care for your mother when she's discharged. Oh, before we do that, is this a good number for you?" She pointed to the paper. "We tried calling and it didn't go through."

"No, I haven't had that number in years." I watched her correct the number and then we set the appointment. Ma was finally going to be integrated back into her lifestyle. Although I was excited to talk about her discharge, I was also nervous to find out how this would work.

"Your Aunt Jess came to visit earlier," Ma mentioned after the woman left.

I looked up from a commercial. "I wondered what time she was coming. She sent a text earlier saying she was in town and then asked for your room number and visiting hours."

"She came this morning. She left not too long before you two got here."

"Dang, wish I would've known. Would've been nice to see her." Aunt Jess, Ma's second oldest sister, had been like a second mother to me. Her house served as the main form of normalcy and stability for Dani and me.

"And my coworker came this morning before Jessica. We had breakfast together."

Amani looked up from her phone and together, we stared at Ma.

"What?" she asked, looking between the two of us.

"I didn't know you had friends!" I added.

"Oh, shut up!" Ma laughed herself into a coughing fit.

I walked over to her end table to hand her the cup of water. "You okay?"

She sipped. "Thank you." When she put her cup down, she smacked me with her good arm.

"Oww! You're still heavy-handed, even after your stroke. Glad you don't do my hair anymore."

"Whatever, that's what you get for making fun of your mother. I have friends. And your sister is coming when she gets off work."

"Full schedule today," I sat back in my chair.

"Tell me about it."

"Well, I'm glad you're not lonely. And soon you'll be outta here. We'll be back tomorrow, too. I'll probably bring Cara since she hasn't been here yet."

"Yes, bring my Carebear up here. That'd be nice."

"Lord, I thank you for helping me to be strong and fearless."
Karen Todd

...they help each other and say to their companions, "Be strong!"
Isaiah 41:6

Sunday, October 14, 2018

When I woke up, I'd missed two calls from Circle of Angels and had one voicemail. I took my phone off *Do Not Disturb* and listened to the voicemail.

A woman's calming, but unsure voice played. *Hi, umm, I'm calling from Circle of Angels. I'm trying to get in contact with the daughter of Karen Todd. If someone can please give me a call back. You can ask for Josh or for the nurse caring for your mom. Umm, please call back as soon as possible. Thank you.*

I headed downstairs. The voicemail didn't sound threatening, so I dialed the number as I prepped my coffee maker. In the basement, I heard Cara playing with Lamar, which made me smile as I waited for someone to pick up.

"Circle of Angels, how can I assist you?"

"Hi, this is Cori Sykes. I missed a couple calls from you and so I'm calling back. I'm supposed to ask for Josh or the nurse caring for Karen Todd."

"Is she in the assisted living or rehabilitation department?"

"Rehab."

"Just a minute."

The transfer felt like a lifetime. I prayed they were calling to reschedule my appointment, although the feeling in my stomach sent off warning bells.

"Rehabilitation," a woman picked up.

"Hi, can I speak to Josh or the nurse caring for Karen Todd? This is her daughter, Cori Sykes, and I missed a couple of calls from here this morning."

The woman's voice lowered. "This is Cori Sykes?"

"Yes."

"Okay," she took a breath. "We were calling to let you know we found your mother unresponsive…"

"What?"

"…in her room last night."

"Oh my God."

"So, we called nine-one-one and she was rushed to the hospital."

"Is she okay?" The woman paused so long I thought we had been disconnected.

"I don't know. You'd have to call the hospital."

"Which one?"

"She was taken to Huber Health."

"Okay." I hung up and my mind went into planning mode overdrive. I was already two hours behind their first call and I truly did not want to think about why Ma hadn't called to let me know she was in the hospital. My mismatched pajamas would suffice and Ma, who cared less about many things, wouldn't give my appearance a second look. I just needed shoes. No, I needed to tell Lamar I was leaving.

I jogged to the top of the basement stairs from the kitchen. "Babe, I gotta go. The nursing home called and said they rushed Ma to the hospital last night."

He responded exactly as I felt. Pensive. Nervous. "Okay." He shuffled in the basement and before I left the top of the stairs I heard him mumble, "Come on, Carebear."

No doubt, he was coming to get information I didn't have. I didn't know if she was in a coma or feeling just fine. The last thing I wanted was for her to be wondering why her family wasn't there. With one shoe in hand and the other on my foot, I saw Lamar's head poke into the kitchen.

He held Carebear on his chest. "What happened?"

"I don't know. They just said they found her unresponsive last night and rushed her to the hospital. So, I'm going to the hospital…see what's going on." I shoved the other shoe on my foot. "Okay, just need my keys." My eyes darted around, looking for my keys, waiting for my brain to catch up to remind me where they were.

Lamar nodded. "Want me to go with you?"

The Clouds Will Catch Me

"I'm good. Stay here with the girls." My phone rang. Circle of Angels was calling back.

"Hello," I answered on the second ring.
"Cori?"
"Yes."
"This is Circle of Angels. I just got off the phone with the hospital. They were calling when we were on the phone."
"Okay."

Lamar stared at me, trying to read my expression while simultaneously trying to keep Carebear quiet.

"I'm sorry to tell you, your mom didn't make it."

Instant tears wet my cheeks. One small statement and none of it made sense. "What?"

"I'm sorry. Your mom died."

"How? I don't understand." My voice cracked along with my heart. "I was just there yesterday. Less than twelve hours ago. She was fine."

Lamar took me into his arms.

"I'm sorry," the woman said.

"What happened?" I tried my best to remain calm. Practice made perfect and I was a pro at that.

"I don't know. But I have the number and a name of the nurse at the hospital for you to call. They've been trying to reach you."

"Okay." I pulled out of Lamar's arms and wrote down the information. The writing on the paper made me want to throw up. I was vaguely aware of Lamar standing near me as I dialed the nurse at the hospital. She was expecting my call.

When the hospital nurse answered, her sincerity was warming, but it did little to soothe me. "Yes, I am sorry for your loss. We've been trying to contact you. Does your number start with five-oh-nine?"

Once again, my number was incorrect in somebody's system. "No, I haven't had that number in years."

"Okay, that was the number listed in your mom's file."

I nodded. Unsure of what to say, I asked, "What happens now? Do I need to come and claim her? I've never been in this situation before."

"Are you your mom's next of kin?
"Yes, she wasn't married and I'm her oldest daughter."

The nurse's instructions were simple: find a funeral home and wait for the organ donation company to call since Ma was an organ donor. Still, I needed verification that Ma was truly gone.

"Can I see her?" There was no way Ma was dead today when she was fine yesterday. The nursing home had the wrong person. The wrong patient. The wrong room. Ma would call any minute to see what time I was coming. Any minute.

"I'd have to call down to the morgue. We had to send her down there because she had been here so long. Let me call you back with an answer, okay?"

"Okay."

I hung up and turned to my husband, lips pressed together in an effort not to melt down. "She's in the morgue."

He allowed me to cry into his shirt until I made myself pull it together. I had to tell Amani and Dani.

Amani was still sleeping. Awful message to wake up to. "Amani," I shook her. "Sweetie, wake up."

Our dog, Foxx, stirred first, opening his eyes and lifting his head. He was getting old and, recently, I'd had the talk with Amani about needing to put him down soon. With the news of Ma that day, I prayed it wouldn't be soon. Our cat, Daisy, also on Amani's bed, stretched out her legs. She was in perfect health.

"Yeah." With her eyes closed, Amani covered the leg sticking out from under the cover and rolled onto her side.

"Open your eyes, I need to tell you something important. And sit up please." She did as she was told, but at a snail's pace. I expected nothing more. Neither of us were morning people.

I took a deep breath. We'd never gone through a death of this magnitude before. I had no idea what to expect, so I braced for whatever came my way.

"The nursing home called this morning. Last night, they found Grandma in her room and she wasn't breathing. They called nine-one-one and she was rushed to the hospital, but, umm…" My heart threatened to thump right out of my chest. I hated saying the words that confirmed Ma's earthly status when I had yet to receive proof.

"Umm, Grandma died. She didn't make it."

We stayed in silence. Me fiddling with my hands. Amani watching the floor. We were frozen until, finally, Amani swiped away a runaway tear. Lamar appeared at Amani's bedroom door with Cara just as I pulled Amani into my arms. Through her tears, she finally asked the question which was already haunting me.

"What happened?"

"I don't know, sweetie. I don't know." We stayed in the moment until I realized I needed to pull away. "I need to call Aunt Dee Dee. Are you going to be okay?"

Amani nodded. "Are you going to be okay, Mom?"

"In time."

I walked into my bedroom with Lamar behind me to break the news to my sister.

"Hey, Co," Dani answered cheerfully. This was going to be worse than I expected.

"Hey, Dani. What are you doing?"

"I just got downtown for work. I'm walking to the building now."

Right. It was Sunday. She worked at the Cleveland Browns Stadium. "Okay, umm, I have bad news." My stomach dropped again and I wondered if I would experience that feeling for the rest of my life whenever I had to tell someone about Ma. "Ma died."

Disbelief instantly replaced her joy. "What?" I could tell by her breathing that she had stopped walking.

"The nursing home called. Said they found her unresponsive, called nine-one-one. She was taken to the hospital and she died."

"But, Co, I was just there. How could she be dead?"

"When were you there?"

"Last night. I left around nine."

"Okay, so you were there after me and Amani. I don't know what time it happened. They said it happened last night, but they didn't call me until seven this morning." She remained silent. "Can you call off and come over?"

Lamar mouthed a message to me. "Lamar said he'll come get you."

Dani provided her location and Lamar left to pick her up. I had more calls to make. The first was to Aunt Jess, who I prayed would be able to help us through this. Thankfully, on her way home the previous night, she had gotten tired and decided to stop at a hotel to rest. After her shock wore off, she promised to get back on the road and come back to be with us.

From there, I called Nicky, my friends, and other aunts and uncles who relayed the news to my cousins. None of the calls lasted long. I had to keep moving. Plus, reliving the tragedy every time I picked up the phone was taking a toll. I was barely getting out the words, "My mom died last night."

By the evening, my house was flooded with family and well-wishers. To make matters worse, Foxx was on a serious decline. We had resorted to wrapping him in blankets and placing him in his bed in front of the space heater just to keep him warm.

"Please, Foxx - I won't let you keep suffering - but please, please, just don't die tonight. I can't take much more."

> "Lord, thank You for helping me to be still and steadfast. I know You know what is best for me."
> Karen Todd

And the God of all grace, who called you to his eternal glory in Christ, after you have suffered a little while, will himself restore you and make you strong, firm and steadfast.
1 Peter 5:10

Monday, October 15, 2018

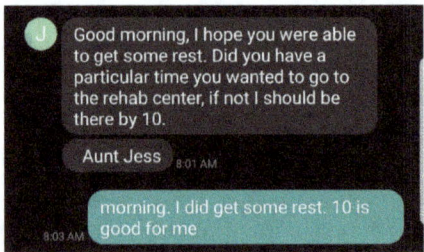

The atmosphere at the nursing home had shifted. No one smiled at us, or at least it felt that way. We were meeting with the nursing manager to receive an explanation of Ma's death. As we waited, I cautioned Dani to keep her temper in check. We desperately wanted answers and the last thing we wanted was for the nursing manager to stop talking and end the meeting.

Thirty minutes later, she rushed toward us. "Sorry about that, I was in a meeting with the nursing director. Sorry for your loss." She shook all of our hands. "I have a conference room where we can talk. Follow me."

She led us to the front of the nursing home and into a conference room that was directly behind the reception area. The nurse, Lamar, Dani, Aunt Jess, and I took our seats around a dark room with a large wooden table.

"Thank you for meeting with us. We were just looking for some information on what happened to our mom. We all," I motioned around the table, "visited her on Saturday and she was fine. Then, on Sunday morning, she was gone. None of that makes sense to us."

She nodded as if she wanted to hurry me along. "Yes, what I know is they went in there and that's when they found her.

They initiated CPR, called nine-one-one, and she was taken to the hospital, where she was pronounced."

That was what she knew, and it was nothing. "So how often do the nurses make their rounds? How long had it been since they had last checked on her?"

Her hands steadied over each other. "I would have to call the nurse that was on duty last night because I wasn't here over the weekend. But typically, they make their rounds at least every two hours. And, of course, they have their call light, if she needed anything in between then, you know…"

I'd almost forgotten about the call light. "Did she pull the call light?"

"I wasn't here, unfortunately, so I would have to call the nurse and get all of those details. But he has proper documentation in his chart and the nurses acted accordingly. They did all they could."

Leaning in her seat, Dani spoke up. "Because I got there around five forty-five and I left around eight thirty--ish. Only one nurse came in. Once. And there was another nurse that came for a little bit because the other nurse took too long."

"Well, all I can say is that if a nurse only came in there once, she was alert and oriented and if she needed anything, she would call."

Dani's eyes pierced the nurse's. "I was there, so I know she was alert. She was alert from the time I was there to the time I left. It's just, there was one nurse that came from around five forty-five…"

"Okay, well again, I wasn't here. I can't answer that."

Feeling as if the nurse was getting edgy, I spoke again. "It was very surprising. We all…my aunt…"

The nurse interrupted again. "It was surprising to all of us."

"…my aunt was there earlier…"

"Dr. Carnegie and Mary Lou too. They were like, 'Whoa'. Completely unexpected."

I did my best to keep my cool. "Did my mom, our mom, complain about chest pain…"

"No, if she had chest pain, it would've been addressed immediately. Probably, she would've been sent out nine-one-one for chest pain. There is nothing documented that she complained of any discomfort, shortness of breath, or anything like that."

"What about her medicine? Did she take all of her medicine that…"

"There is nothing documented that she did not."

I gritted my teeth, tired of the nurse's disrespect. "Okay. So you're saying that you don't know if she pulled the help cord?"

"No, I can't answer that because I wasn't here."

"Okay," I stretched out my tight neck. "Is there someone that was here that we could talk to right now?"

"That would be night shift and they're not here during the day."

Dani leaned into the table. "Okay, because it's like, you're just not giving us the answers that we're asking for. You know what I mean?"

The nurse's face tightened. "Well, I trust my nurses to document properly. All the nurses acted accordingly. As far as when she pulled the call light or how often she did, I can't answer that. It would be one of the STNAs answering the call lights."

This was turning out to be a huge waste of time. We had a funeral to plan and this woman was playing "Ring Around the Rosie" with us. "Okay, well do you know what time they first called me? You say she was found at four fifty-five that morning, but according to my call log the first call I received from Circle of Angels was at seven in the morning. That's two hours later--"

She spoke fast, "The note indicates they tried calling several times, but the voicemail was indicating that it was full, I believe."

"My voicemail is not full. I know you all had the wrong number originally…"

"Then that must have been what it was. I know that their note indicates that they tried several times. And then the hospital did as well."

"I corrected the number here, when I was here on Saturday because someone was going to schedule a meeting with me for the following Thursday for after-care instructions. It's just like, the first voicemail I got was at seven and not that I could've saved my mom or anything like that, but it's a little disturbing that it happened at four fifty-five and I didn't receive a voicemail until seven o'clock."

"That would be disturbing. I can't answer that for you."

Dani stopped herself from slamming her hand on the table. "So who can?"

A short stare off commenced before the nurse became visibly flustered. Just then, the records department walked in, handing us paperwork to sign for the records that we hoped would provide more information. "If you pick them up, it's about forty-eight hours. If you want us to mail them to you, it just depends on how long the mail takes."

My voice had diminished significantly. "Thank you. Will there be someone here that can go over the records with me if there are things that I don't understand, like medical terms or lingo?"

The nurse spoke again. "I'd have to check with my director of nursing. In the meantime, I'll reach out to Josh and see if he can give more information. Find out what happened with the incorrect number because clearly, they were calling the wrong number. Who did you give the correct number to? Do you remember?"

"No. It was a heavyset black woman with glasses. Shorter hair."

"I don't know who that could be."

Tension brewed into my shoulders. "Does this happen often? And I know that's probably something you guys will not answer."

"A code? That's completely unpredictable."

"And you said the nurse did administer CPR?"

"Yes. When they went into the room, she was discolored, they did a head to toe, a sternal rub, that's when they found there was no pulse, and they initiated CPR. They intubated her, to get her back so that tells me there was still hope. Because when she left here, she had a pulse. She was pronounced at the hospital."

"Do you know how long it took the ambulance to get here?"

"Usually the ambulance is here within a few to five minutes. They're right down the road. It's the City of Mandover."

I was out of questions, patience and my mind. "So, when I come back for the records, you said you will have somebody here to go over them with me?"

"Yes, I'll speak with my director of nursing and see what we're liable for legally." As someone walked in with the box of Ma's belongings, she rose from the table. "I'm very sorry for your loss."

We all walked to the parking lot, ingesting the lack of information given. The place that I'd previously praised was a joke and I wished I had paid more attention to Ma's nervous concerns.

"They're liars." Dani broke the silence between us. "How could she not know if Ma pulled the help cord? I'm gonna contact Tim. He's a lawyer who comes to my club. He'll help us."

"Yeah, it's time to get a lawyer," I agreed. "This is ridiculous. And I bet she was late meeting us because the director was telling her what she could and could not tell us."

Aunt Jess remained silent, nodding when necessary. "They know more than they're telling us. Listen, I'm going to head home. If you need anything, and I mean anything, don't hesitate to call me. And let me know when you get those records."

Dani and I agreed in unison and hugged her goodbye.

"I love you two. And again, regardless of what it is, call me if you need anything."

"Okay." Dani and I hopped in my car with Ma's purse. Having it with us broke a bigger piece of my heart. Things were getting real.

"Proclaim, declare, and decree God's goodness in your life and His power to recover all."
Karen Todd

You will surely forget your trouble, recalling it only as waters gone by.
Job 11:16

Thursday, October 18, 2018

Before I second-guessed my decision, I looked away from Foxx's large, pain-filled eyes. They'd grown red around the rims and spoke of the pain I knew he could no longer handle. Each time I looked at him, I became an emotional wreck, laughing at memories one moment and crying the next.

Lamar hated animals prior to us dating. But, at that moment, he pressed his lips together to avoid crying. Throughout the years, they had enjoyed one of the most entertaining love-hate relationships, arguing in the morning and breaking bread together during dinner.

He came closer and asked, "You ready?"

My eyes watered but I held the tears back. I wasn't ready to cry just yet. "Yeah."

And I believed Foxx was, too. The night before, I'd taken him on one last joyride in Ma's car. She had always joked about taking him on car rides, so in honor of them both, I completed the task.

The ride to the vet was too short and, when I checked him in, my emotions were raw. The secretary we'd grown to know over the last twelve years provided a smile of pity. "It's time, huh?"

I nodded to avoid speaking.

"Alright. Have a seat and we'll get you into a room."

Inside, I watched Foxx drag across the room, all traces of his original spunk obsolete. The question of whether I'd waited too long or had taken the leap too soon, circled my mental drain while I simultaneously attempted to process the veterinary technician's explanation of the upcoming procedure. Essentially, Foxx would just naturally go to sleep. Only this time, he would not be waking up.

I chose not to be in the room when it happened. With everything we'd just been through, I couldn't bear to watch him take his last breath. After the veterinary technician left, we said our goodbyes and rubbed his head one last time.

Anger coated my skin's surface. The wrong phrase or touch from anyone could land them on the wrong side of right with me. As I walked into the nursing home to retrieve the records, I noted how everything seemed exactly the same, as if Ma hadn't just died. I stepped up to the counter, remaining calm, but prepared to lose it all if prompted.

A young female called me to the counter. "How can I help you?"

"I'm here to pick up the records for Karen Todd."

She turned to the counter behind her and spun around with a heavy white envelope in her hand. "Here they are. You were supposed to pick them up yesterday," she smiled.

I shook my head and rolled my eyes. "No, I wasn't supposed to pick them up yesterday. Someone was supposed to call me to let me know they were ready to be picked up. Of course, no one bothered to do so."

The girl took a step back while I opened the contents. It was riddled with medical lingo, as expected. The only sense I could make of it was Ma's name. "When I requested these records, I was told someone would be here to go over them with me. I'm not in the medical field so I don't understand what most of this is saying."

Another young female employee, who had been standing to the side, plastered a smile on her face and called over the next person. The line behind me was growing and I had no intent on leaving without getting what I needed.

The employee I had been talking to raised her eyebrows and spoke slowly, "Let me go get someone. I'll be right back."

A couple of minutes later, she returned with a middle-aged woman with long brown hair, who seemed to hold a more senior role. She busied herself with waiting for the visitors to clear before calling me over to the side counter.

"You're looking for someone to help you, right? What do you need help with?"

"All of this. I need someone to go over this with me." My fingers flipped through the pages, allowing them to fall back down.

She looked at the file and said in a calm voice, "What specifically do you want to know?"

My internal rubber band immediately snapped. My heart rate and voice rose in synchrony. "Everything! I'm not a doctor. I don't understand this. I want someone to go through this and explain it to me."

The woman, who was a professional at keeping her cool, maintained her composure, which I hated. How many times had she gone through this before with other families?

"We don't have anyone available to do that right now."

"That's unacceptable! When I came up here and talked to the nurse manager, she said someone would go over the records with me and now you're saying no one can."

"I'm sorry, but no one is currently available. When I spoke to the nurse manager, she said they told you everything at your meeting…"

With the way my heart skipped around in my chest at that moment, I was pretty sure I was about to have a heart attack. "They told me NOTHING! She didn't know this. She didn't know that. Her answer to almost every question was, 'I don't know. I wasn't here.' How does that answer my questions?"

People around the facility stopped to watch our exchange. I noticed family members who were visiting the residents and that gave me the ammunition to continue. "This place is so unprofessional! And do you know someone from here called my mother's phone yesterday to see how she was doing since she was released? Do you know how it feels to get a call like that after your mother has died?"

"That's awful. Do you know who it was?"

"No! I was so shocked that I couldn't even process what had just happened. When I told them that my mom had died here, they hung up on me."

"Your mom did not die here. She was alive when she left."

As far as I was concerned, Circle of Angels had lost all credibility and there wasn't one person I would trust in that facility. "How do you know that? Are you authorized to pronounce death?"

"We absolutely can pronounce death."

"So, you're telling me that you're a medical facility that can pronounce death but yet, you don't have one medical person available to go over these records with me?"

The woman did not respond, but an older woman, also behind the counter, nodded her head in my defense. I had a feeling that everyone in the facility was aware of the drama surrounding Ma's death and all eyes were on me. At that moment, I fought for Ma. I fought for my daughters. My sister. My husband. And all of Ma's siblings who had been denied another phone call with her.

"My mother was fifty-nine years old." I said, attempting to calm my cracking voice. A stubborn tear ran down my face and I didn't bother to wipe it away.

"I understand what you're going through, my mother..."

I did not care about her mother. She knew nothing about my struggle. "I don't even know what time my mother died."

"The hospital can tell you that."

"I've been there!" I slammed my hand down on the file. Over the past four days, I'd traveled to Huber Healths's main campus, requested records from all of her doctors, and spoken to organ donation company.

"No one knows anything and no one will tell me anything. I'm just trying to find out what happened to my mom."

The woman's eyes teared up and remorse clouded my vision. Although Ma had her own streak of mean, she'd raised us to do better. I lowered my voice. "I don't mean to take out my anger on you, but you have to understand where I'm coming from."

She nodded.

"Is there someone else I can speak to? The medical director?"

She swallowed and her eyes cleared. "He's not here right now."

"When will he be here?"

"I don't know. He runs a very busy practice outside of here."

As quickly as I had calmed, my anger began rising once more. She had to be kidding. The medical director of this facility wasn't here because he was too busy running an outside practice. "Well, maybe he shouldn't be *directing* this place if he doesn't have time to be here. What's his number? I'll give him a call."

"I can't give that to you."

"What's his email?"

"I can't give that to you either."

I shook my head and smirked. "Well, you give him my name, number, and email." I waited while she wrote it down. "And you tell him that I will be up here every day until he calls me."

If the woman in the background wasn't already standing, I believe she would've given me a standing ovation. I walked out with my head held high. They had no idea who they were dealing with.

Once in my car, I called Lamar and updated him, explaining why I was happy not to be in jail. He listened with an open heart and, after ending the call, I made my way to Huber Health's satellite campus. It was the last location on my list and I prayed that I would be able to receive answers.

After I explained the situation at the front desk, I was sent to the morgue. Television had always made me believe that morgues were cold rooms with greyish-blue walls, metal tables, and toe tags. But there I sat, in a waiting room with comfortable chairs and artwork on the walls.

"Cori Sykes."

I made my way to the security guard, who crossed my name off the sheet on his clipboard. "My mom, Karen Todd, was brought here a few days ago. I'm trying to find out when exactly she died. Right now, I'm not really sure. Could have been the thirteenth or the fourteenth."

The man, void of all emotion, towered over me in his grey uniform. He stared as if waiting for me to say more, then reached for a binder sitting just out of my view. "That name sounds familiar. We weren't able to contact you, right?" He stopped flipping through the pages to look at me.

I avoided eye contact. "Yes."

A beat stuck in the air before he swallowed and resumed turning the pages. "Here it is. Karen Todd. Died October fourteenth at five forty-six a.m."

My knees weakened and I gripped the counter. I had a date and time. I was finally getting somewhere, but I craved more. "What else does it say? Does it say how she died?"

"I wouldn't know that. You could go up to the emergency room department. Her records are there and they can tell you more."

The satisfaction from the minute details hit hard and I would've smiled under different circumstances. If someone would've told me that one day I would feel a sense of gratitude for the person that provided Ma's date and time of death, I would've "knocked the sense into them", as Ma had threatened to do to me many times.

"Thank you."

I made my way to the emergency room through a haze that felt like a mixture of pain and glory. A petite nurse escorted me to an open room where she pulled up Ma's information on a computer.

"Have a seat, honey."

Her soft voice seemed to lower my blood pressure and I told her everything, much like I would a therapist. In turn, she told me everything she knew.

Ma was picked up from Circle of Angels by the City of Mandover EMS. They worked on her for forty-five minutes and made an unsuccessful attempt to give her life-saving medicine through an IV. Unfortunately, they hadn't been able to locate a vein. When they arrived at Huber Health satellite campus at 5:45, a doctor pronounced her death at 5:46. They called the emergency number on file repeatedly, but it was my old cell phone number. At least they had tried.

Cori Sykes

"Thank you, Lord, for being a comforter."
Karen Todd

For just as we share abundantly in the sufferings of Christ, so also our comfort abounds through Christ.
2 Corinthians 1:5

Tuesday, October 23, 2018

We finally made it to the day of the funeral and we were in good spirits. Somehow, we had made it through the viewing of Ma's body, picking out her last outfit, and creating the program. None of them were things we wanted to do, but they were all the things we had to do.

To honor her, we did little things like rinse our hair in the color plum and wear plum lipstick, as this was her favorite color. The service was a blur, but I was thankful to see so many of the friends we never knew she had, attend the service. Her coworkers, new and old, reflected on how she was a caring, thoughtful, and joyful person that, regardless of how she was feeling physically, emotionally, or mentally, gave encouragement, laughter, and love to others.

During the service, when the pastor opened the floor for comments, no one moved. As I waited, I heard Ma's voice in my ears. *What? You don't have anything to say about me?*

I rose from my seat. Lamar started to accompany me, but I assured him I would be fine. "I know you all know my mom, but you don't *really* know her." I laughed. "Growing up, my mom was crazy. Over time, she did change, but I didn't notice. I still saw her as crazy and kind of mean and that's not who I wanted her to be. I wanted her to be different. More like Phylicia Rashad. The weird thing is, she had already changed from the crazy old lady into something different; I just couldn't see it. In a way, I lost out because I didn't accept her for her. My grandparents died when I was a little girl. My dad left when I was a baby. My brother died when I was three. My mom, before I'm thirty-five. I've lost a lot of people too soon. It's honestly

Cori Sykes

not fair, but I've learned that if you wait for people to change to who you want them to be, you'll miss out on loving them as the unique individuals that God built them to be."

Lamar squeezed my shoulders when I returned to my seat and whispered, "I was gonna say something, but I can't top that."

I snickered and shook my head.

At the cemetery, overcast skies and cold winds tortured us as soon as we stepped out of the limo. "You couldn't have given us a nicer day, Ma?" I looked to the sky and wrapped myself tighter in my peacoat.

"I know. Thanks a lot, Karen Todd," Dani added, trying not to sink into the soft ground in her heels.

Amani, also shivering, chuckled. "Remember when I almost fell into the grave at Uncle Trent's funeral?"

"Don't remind me," I huffed. "And please watch your step here. That's all we need is for you to fall into the grave with your grandma."

Next to the casket, Lamar shook his head and pulled Dani and me to his sides, trying to keep us warm. Amani, now opposite of us, stood close to her biological father.

The minister looked at me and asked, "Shall I begin?"

I nodded. "Yes."

Five minutes into the short graveside service, the sun appeared from behind the clouds. Lamar gently elbowed my side to get my attention, but I had already noticed what caught his and Dani's sight.

Illuminated on top of Ma's casket was our three shadows. Dani's, Lamar's and my silhouette glowed in breathtaking beauty, just as the wind stilled. No one else seemed to notice the abrupt change in weather and I knew it was a sign directly from Ma. She was happy where she was and still watched over us. Today, she was our warmth.

Under my breath, I whispered, "Thanks, Ma."

"Make the choice to rejoice."
Karen Todd

The Clouds Will Catch Me

I have told you these things, so that in me you may have peace. In this world you will have trouble. But take heart! I have overcome the world.

John 16:33

About Vibes: We are a hybrid publishing company that believes writers should only have to worry about writing. Meaning, you write your book, we'll do the rest.

To learn more about us, our authors, and their books, please visit us at

Writeandvibe.com | Fb & IG @writeandvibe

www.ingramcontent.com/pod-product-compliance
Lightning Source LLC
Chambersburg PA
CBHW071423070526
44578CB00003B/678